LIFE SKILLS

CRAFTY CREATIVITY

Sue Barraclough

Heinemann
LIBRARY

www.heinemannlibrary.co.uk
Visit our website to find out more information about Heinemann Library books.

To order:
☎ Phone +44 (0) 1865 888066
🖷 Fax +44 (0) 1865 314091
🖳 Visit www.heinemannlibrary.co.uk

Edited by Harriet Milles and Adam Miller
Designed by Philippa Jenkins and Artisitix
Original illustrations © Capstone Global Library
   Limited 2008
Illustrated by KJA Artists
Picture research by Elizabeth Alexander and
   Maria Joannou
Originated by Heinemann Library
Printed and bound in China by South China
   Printing Company Ltd.

ISBN 978 0 431112 70 1
13 12 11 10 09
10 9 8 7 6 5 4 3 2 1

British Library Cataloguing in Publication Data
Barraclough, Sue
   Crafty creativity. - (Life skills)
   1. Handicraft - Juvenile literature 2. Creative ability -
   Juvenile literature
   I. Title
   745.5
A full catalogue record for this book is available from the British Library.

Acknowledgements

We would like to thank the following for permission to reproduce photographs: © Alamy/Bob Elam p. **16**; © Alamy/Elizabeth Whiting & Associates p. **37**; © Capstone Global Library pp. **9**, **40** bottom, **45**, **47**; © Capstone Global Library/MM Studios pp. **11**, **20**, **21**, **22** top, **22** bottom, **23**, **25**, **27**, **29**, **30**, **32**, **42**, **46** top, **46** bottom; © Getty Images pp. **48** (Robert Harding World Imagery), **12** (Taxi/Lee Strickland); © Istockphoto/Rick Rhay p. **36** left; © Photolibrary/Photographic Dan Gair/Index Stock Imagery p. **4**; © Rex Features/Paul Cooper p. **39**; © Shutterstock pp. **34** (Amy Walters), **40** top (David Hsu), **34** (Fritz Kocher), **7** (Jan Hopgood), **36** top (Mary E. McCabe), **45** (Stephen Coburn), **34** (Victoria Alexandrova), **34** (ViZualStudio) **40** bottom (Yuri Arcurs), **28**, **36** right; © Topham Picturepoint/Bob Daemmrich p. **15**.

Cover photograph of a young woman holding giant knitting needles reproduced with permission of © Corbis/Cultura.

The cards featured on page 42 were made by Sarah Shannon.

We would like to thank Joanna Hinton-Malivoire and Katie Miller for their invaluable help in the preparation of this book.

Every effort has been made to contact copyright holders of material reproduced in this book. Any omissions will be rectified in subsequent printings if notice is given to the publishers.

Contents

Some words are printed in bold, **like this**. You can find out what they mean by looking in the glossary.

A craft is making something useful or decorative by hand, using simple tools. Most crafts need specific skills and techniques, equipment, and often materials to create a particular product. Unlike items made in huge quantities by factory machines, something made by hand is unique.

CRAFT SKILLS

This book will teach you simple skills for a mix of crafts. It is a brief introduction to the world of craft and should help you find out which types of crafts appeal to you. The aim is to aid understanding of skills, materials, and terminology, as well as provide ideas and inspiration. Hopefully, you will then want to find out more, and develop your own designs and ways of working.

Different by design

Each craft has a set of instructions or a series of steps to follow in order to make something. Each person follows the instructions to make a similar product. The great thing is that each person can follow the same steps and make small changes to create something unique. Once you are confident about what you are doing, you can make more changes to create something new and different.

Traditional crafts create useful and beautiful items using skills passed down through the generations.

A skilled craftsperson or **artisan** uses the right tools, and uses them safely and well. A crucial part of every craft is choosing the best tools for the job.

Ideas and inspiration

For any craft, having a collection of ideas and styles is inspiring. Collect beads, fabrics, printed papers, or pictures from magazines, and add them to a poster board or a large notebook so you'll never be short of inspiration. Some things to remember:

- Keep an open mind. Experiment, think, plan, doodle, and play around with ideas.

- Ideas or skills you have learned for one craft may be useful for another. For example, you might use embroidery stitches on a piece of knitting or a string of beads to decorate a fabric bag.

- Keep pictures and sketches of anything you like; you don't need to know how you will use them. Seeing how other people have used materials and colour will help you decide what you think works.

Colour in craft

Choosing colours that work together is not always easy, so understanding how a colour wheel works helps. **Primary colours** are red, yellow, and blue. **Secondary colours** are made by mixing primary colours together. On a colour wheel, similar colours are side by side, and different colours are opposite each other. Looking at colours in nature is a useful way to see how colours can be combined. For example, the reds and oranges of a sunset are similar colours. But the red of a tulip and its green stem and leaves are **complementary** colours that are opposite each other on the colour wheel. Understanding colour similarities and differences is the key to making colour choices.

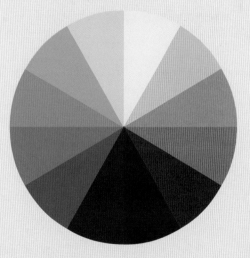

A colour wheel is a handy tool when choosing colour combinations.

Needlecraft

Sewing is an important life skill. Whether you need to sew on a button or mend a favourite shirt, there won't always be someone around to do it for you. Some simple sewing skills will also mean you can try some cool **customizing** projects.

CUSTOMIZING YOUR CLOTHES

Fashions change all the time so having the sewing skills to adapt your clothes to stay with the trends, and to suit you, can only be a good thing. Colour, fabrics, and decorative details can all be used to update clothes and keep your wardrobe cool. Study fashion magazines to see how different designers use colour, texture, patterns, and other details in their clothes.

Finding your own style

Understanding how clothes are made and learning about different fabrics is crucial to finding your own style. Charity shops are full of cheap clothes for you to experiment with. If you decide you don't like the end result, at least you have still given money to a good cause.

Storing sewing equipment

Keeping your sewing supplies in good order will make sewing more fun. If your sewing basket is a muddle of knotted threads and jumbled fabrics, you'll never be able to find anything. The best sewing box is one where you can find things quickly, so you can get on with the business of creating something.

Try to create a separate compartment or drawer for storing interesting items that you may have collected over time. You are more likely to feel motivated if your sewing kit is filled with inspirational odds and ends.

TIP

Before you throw away old clothes save any beautiful buttons and scraps of fabric. Also keep favourite lace trimmings or other decorative items, as you may be able to use them again in unexpected ways. The clever use of unusual buttons or trim can often transform a mundane article into something beautiful and unique.

Pincushion

Use two contrasting coloured, textured, or patterned fabrics, but make sure the fabrics are a similar thickness. Put a small bowl or a saucer on the pieces of fabric and draw around them to make two circles. Cut out the fabric circles. Put the right sides together and sew a 1.3-centimetre (half-inch) seam all the way round, leaving 2.5 centimetres (1 inch) open. Turn so the right sides show and stuff the cushion shape with cotton wool or **batting**. Sew up the gap. Decorate with stitches, buttons, or sequins.

Needle book

Make a needle book for storing your needles by cutting out a rectangle of felt. Fold it in half like a book. Then cut out three or four slightly smaller rectangles of a thinner fabric to make the "pages" of the book. Put the pages inside the felt cover, and use a large needle and wool to sew three or four stitches to hold the pages in. You could knit a cover for this as a simple knitting project (see page 19).

Sewing kit basics

A sewing kit needs a few essential items:

- A packet of needles in various sizes
- Cotton thread – black and white are most useful
- Dressmaking shears or sharp scissors
- A tape measure
- A box of steel pins
- Hooks, eyes, and poppers
- Buttons
- Safety pins
- A thimble for pushing needles through thick fabric.

Sewing Stitches

Learning a few simple stitches will help you tackle most sewing tasks. However, if you want to add decoration to your project, you can teach yourself some basic embroidery stitches. Embroidery is using decorative stitching to create pictures or patterns.

Embroidery stitches

Stem stitch – to make an outline for items or patterns on fabric.

Appliqué stitch – use for sewing on patches of material. Keep the stitches close to raw edges to stop them fraying.

Useful stitches

Hemming stitch – use for taking up skirts and trousers so that the stitches don't show.

Back stitch – use to sew fabric firmly together, or to make bold or thin lines.

Chain stitch – a series of loops for borders or flower stems.

Knot stitch – a simple stitch that adds dots of colour.

 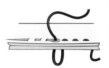

Slip stitch – use to make an invisible seam between two folded edges.

Running stitch – a series of short stitches that can be used for hems or seams. You can also use it to add simple decorative details.

Lazy Daisy – for simple flower and petal shapes.

Satin stitch – a versatile stitch that can be adapted to create many different designs.

Blanket stitch – ideal for sewing along the edge of fabrics to stop them fraying.

Basting stitch – use to temporarily hold pieces of fabric together.

Sewing on buttons

Sometimes cheap or dull buttons can let a garment down, but you can often transform it simply by sewing on new buttons:

1. Close the garment so you can mark the position of the buttons. If you are replacing buttons, cut the old ones off leaving a thread behind to mark their position.

2. Thread your needle with a length of matching thread and make a knot in the end.

3. Push the needle through the first hole and then back through the next. Sew in and out of the holes at least six or seven times.

4. Wind the thread round and round under the button a few times.

5. Push the needle back through to the back of the button and knot.

Don't be tempted to make your thread too long. It will just get tangled and knotted as you try to pull it through the fabric you are sewing. You may think that a long thread will save you time but it won't!

TIP

QUICK CRAFT

Simple Brooch

Sew a simple brooch. Roughly cut out a flower or other **graphic** element from a piece of thick fabric (e.g. curtain fabric). Glue the flower shape to felt and cut carefully around the edges. Stitch round the edge using blanket stitch.

You can also stitch on beads or sequins, or sew some simple stitches such as knot stitches. Glue to a brooch fastening or even a safety pin (a small patch of fabric glued over the back of the pin will hold it in place).

TRANSFORMING T-SHIRTS

If you have an old T-shirt with a graphic or design that you love and are sorry to lose, save it! Simply cut out the design and transfer it to a brand new T-shirt. Cheap department stores sell plain T-shirts that you can transform.

New life for an old T-shirt

You will need:

- A plain T-shirt
- A design or graphic you want to use again
- Fabric glue
- Pins and scissors
- Needle and coloured thread

T-shirt surgery

Cut out the picture or decoration you want to save from the old T-shirt, making sure you leave a border of about 0.6 centimetres (¼ inch) around it. Position it on the new T-shirt, and hold it in place with a pin or fabric glue. Sew blanket stitch in a contrasting thread all the way around the patch.

Inside-out patch

For an interesting variation, you could cut out the design or decoration leaving a 1.3-centimetre (½-inch) border around it. Think about where you want the design to be on the new T-shirt. Then pinch a piece of fabric right in the middle of this area and cut

a small hole. Put the piece of material underneath the T-shirt so you can see the centre of the design through the hole. Use a pin to hold the material there. Then turn the T-shirt inside out. Use more pins to secure the material firmly in place while you sew around the edge.

Turn the T-shirt the right way round again. Carefully cut away the material using the small hole as your starting point, leaving about 0.6 centimetres (¼ inch) of material to frame the new image.

QUICK CRAFT

Tie Dye

To give an old T-shirt a retro, "hippie" look, try the tie-dye effect. First lay the shirt out flat on a table or work surface. Pinch the centre, and lift it slowly upwards. Run your other hand down the T-shirt, gathering it together in folds. Tightly wind a rubber band around the shirt, about 5 cm from the top. Add more rubber bands down the length of the T-shirt, spaced at roughly 5 cm apart. Soak the T-shirt in a fabric dye for about 20 minutes. Wearing protective gloves, remove the T-shirt from the dye, remove the rubber bands, rinse, and dry. Visit http://crafts.kaboose.com/tie-dyeing.html for more great tie-dye ideas.

Other simple ideas for customizing T-shirts:

- Sew crystals or sequins along the neck or the straps of a vest top.
- Sew beads or sequins on flowers or other graphics to add interest and texture.
- Dye white cotton T-shirts in bright colours. Try **tie-dye** (see box on page 10) or **batik** patterns.
- Make longer sleeves into cap sleeves by cutting and hemming.

TRY THIS!

Stitching on a line of colourful beads is another quick and easy way to transform an old T-shirt.

USING A SEWING MACHINE

If you own, or can borrow a sewing machine there are other sewing projects you can try. You will be able to make things much faster using a sewing machine. It is possible to do most simple projects on a machine that does only a simple straight stitch; you don't need a fancy machine!

How a sewing machine works

It is a good idea to understand how a sewing machine works so that you can get the best out of it. Basically, the needle pushes the thread through the fabric, catching a second thread from a **bobbin** under the "throat plate" in the base of the machine. This loops the two threads together to form a strong stitch.

Practising skills

Practise using the different stitches on your machine on scraps of material. Try sewing in straight lines and then see if you can curve the stitches around in a smooth line. Don't start sewing your actual clothing until you feel you are in control of the machine.

Threading a sewing machine can be fiddly, but practise makes perfect!

Getting it Right

Make sure you read the manual carefully before you begin to use a new sewing machine. Pay close attention to any safety instructions. Before you start any project, test a small piece of the fabric you are using first to make sure you get the tension (the tightness of the stitches) right. Use a sharp needle and good quality thread for each project.

Quick and easy bag

You will need:
90 cm (35 ins) of thick fabric, such as denim, canvas, or upholstery, matching thread, scissors, tape measure.

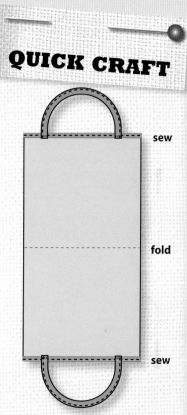

❶ For the bag, measure and cut a long rectangle 76 by 30 cm (30 by 12 ins). For the handles, measure and cut two more rectangles 51 by 15 cm (20 by 6 ins).

❸ To make the bag, sew a 1.3-cm (½-ins) seam along the short ends of the rectangle. Sew the handles about 7.6 cm (3 ins) in from the edges on the seam.

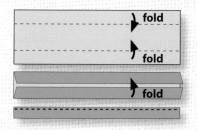

❷ To make the handles, fold the long edges of the rectangle into the middle, then fold the whole thing in half. Pin and sew together along the long open edge.

❹ Fold the rectangle in half with the good sides together and sew down the two long sides. Turn the bag the right way out, and your bag is ready to use.

13

MASTERING SKILLS

Begin by sewing very simple pieces such as bags or cushion covers. If you rush out to buy complicated patterns and expensive fabrics before you have mastered the basics, you may go wrong and your time and materials will be wasted. As a beginner, choose projects that are quick and easy to finish. These will give you a sense of achievement and build up your confidence. To fine-tune your skills, practise making simple items as gifts for friends. If you experiment with different materials and fabrics, you will learn what works by trial and error.

Getting ideas

If you have access to the Internet you will find hundreds of websites featuring ideas and inspiration (and even patterns to print out and use) for all sorts of cool stuff. If you take the time to plan and research ideas, you'll be more likely to make something spectacular that you will want to use or wear all the time.

Picking the right fabrics

If you are choosing clothes from a charity shop to customize, it's worth checking the labels to find out what materials they are made from. Clothes made from natural fabrics such as **silk**, cotton, **linen**, and wool will wash and wear well. **Artificial** fabrics look great when they are new, but will tend to sag and fade after a few washes.

Getting it Wrong

The position or **proportion** of any decorative details is vital for the success of your design. If you add big, heavy buttons to a tiny T-shirt the material will just sag. Or if you add tiny sequins where they can't be seen you'll have wasted your time. Think carefully about decorations you are adding.

When choosing fabrics, remember that some materials are easier to work with than others. Silks can be slippery and hard to handle. Leather needs special needles and very strong thread. For beginners, cotton is cheaper and easier to work with.

Quilting and other sewing crafts

Quilting is a very popular craft. It is a form of patchwork, using three layers of fabric: the top layer, which is usually made up of pieces of fabric sewn together to form a pattern; the middle layer, which is soft padding material; and the bottom layer, which is usually plain. Quilting is stitching the layers together and it can be done by hand or by machine.

Wearing a thimble whilst you sew your quilt makes pushing the needle through layers of fabric much less painful!

Yarn Craft

Yarn is a long, strong thread that is formed by spinning and twisting fibres such as animal wool, cotton, fur, or even acrylics. The yarn can be knitted to make sweaters, hats, scarves, gloves, and a whole range of accessories. Knitting uses two needles to loop and weave the yarn together.

Knitting to go

The great thing about knitting is that you can do it anywhere. Once you have mastered the basics, you can knit while you travel on a bus or train, in a waiting room, or while you watch TV.

Knitting needles

Knitting needles are usually made from metal, wood, or plastic. The pointed end is the knitting part and the knob on the end stops the knitting from slipping off. Needles come in a range of different sizes, and the size relates to how thick they are, 2mm being the thinnest. Thicker needles create bigger stitches. It is important to use the right size needles if you are following a pattern, otherwise your finished garment will not fit you.

Most knitters find the knitting process calming and relaxing.

Useful knitting tools

- *A row counter* – helps keep a count of how many rows you have knitted

- *Needle guards* – when you put knitting away, they stop stitches falling off and also stop the needles sticking into you. You can use old wine bottle corks.

- *Small sharp scissors* – for cutting yarn and trimming loose ends

- *Darning or tapestry needles* – use these large needles to sew pieces of knitting together

- *Tape measure* – for checking sizes and knitting tension

- *A crochet hook* – for adding fringes.

- *A bag with handles* – big enough to fit your needles, wool, pattern, and other knitting equipment.

Types of yarn

Visit the yarn section in a shop and you'll be amazed by the variety of colours and textures. There are **natural fibres** such as wool, mohair, cotton, silk, and linen, and these are often **blended** or mixed together to create different textures. Wool, which is the most widely used yarn, is made from sheep's wool. Other yarns such as cashmere, mohair, and angora are made from goat's wool.

There are also new eco-friendly yarns such as banana silk yarn, made from the stalks and leaves of banana plants, as well as yarns made from bamboo.

Artificial yarns are usually cheaper. These yarns are made from materials such as acrylic and viscose. Artificial yarns may be blended with natural fibres to make them softer.

A ball of yarn usually has a label that says what the yarn is made of and whether it is natural or artificial fibres. It usually gives washing instructions, the size of needles to use, the colour or shade, and lots of other useful information.

DID YOU KNOW?

In the past, knitting was the pastime of shepherds watching their flocks, or sailors on long voyages.

HOW TO KNIT

There are two simple stitches to master first: the knit stitch and the purl stitch. Before you can try either of them, however, you need to know how to knit the first row of stitches, which is called casting on.

Casting on

1 Wind the yarn around your finger to make a loop, and then pull the yarn back through the loop to make a **slip knot**. Slip this "stitch" on to the knitting needle.

2 Hold the needle with the slip knot in your left hand. Put the right needle into the stitch and wind the yarn under and over the needle from right to left.

3 Pull the yarn through the stitch and loop this through and onto the left-hand needle, too.

4 Then put the right needle between the two stitches and wind the yarn round again. Pull the yarn through and slip onto the left needle. Carry on like this until you have the number of stitches you need.

The knit stitch

1 To make a knit stitch, keep the yarn at the back and put the right needle through the first stitch on the left needle. The movement goes left to right, and front to back.

2 Wrap the yarn around the right needle and pull the loop back through the stitch.

3 Slip this new stitch off the left needle and on to the right.

The purl stitch

1 To make purl stitch, keep the yarn at the front and put the right needle into the front of the first stitch, going back to front and right to left.

2 Wrap the yarn around the right needle, pull the loop through.

3 Slip the stitch off the left needle and on to the right.

Casting off

1 Casting off is making a neat edge that will not come undone. Knit two stitches, then using the left-hand needle tip, take the first stitch and lift it over the second stitch.

2 Then slide if off the needle.

3 Now knit another stitch and repeat until only one stitch remains on your left-hand needle. Cut your yarn and pass the tail through your last stitch, pulling it tight.

TIP

Beginner knitters sometimes make their stitches too tight. At first, try to focus on wrapping the yarn more loosely to make sure this doesn't happen. New knitters often cast off too tightly, too. It might help to use a slightly bigger needle for casting off. If you are left-handed you probably won't have a problem with these instructions. However, if you do there are books and lots of websites with clear instructions, and hints and tips for the left-handed knitter.

KNITTING A SCARF

A scarf is another perfect project for a novice knitter. It allows you to practise knit and purl stitches. By making scarves for your friends, you will gain even more practice. If you can't find the wool listed in the pattern ask for help in your local wool shop, and they should be able to recommend a similar type of wool to use.

TIP

If you notice you have dropped a stitch, don't panic and unravel it all. Just go back as far as the dropped stitch and start again. There are many ways to pick up a dropped stitch; check in a knitting book or on the Internet to find out how.

This hat and scarf set is an easy project for a beginner. →

THE SCARF PATTERN

You will need:

12 mm knitting needles, 2 balls of Sirdar®
Denim Ultra wool (use the rest for the hat
on page 22).

- Cast on 12 stitches
- Rows 1-6 – knit
- Row 7 – purl*
- Row 8 – knit
- Repeat last two rows once
- Row 11 – knit
- Repeat last row five times**
- Rows 7 to 16 create the pattern
  and repeat * to ** 13 times.
- Next row – knit
- Repeat last row five times
- Cast off

The asterisk (*) in a pattern is used
to indicate rows of knitting that
need to be repeated.

Learning to knit evenly

While you are learning to knit, focus
on trying to knit evenly. If you don't
knit evenly, your knitting will look
lumpy and bumpy. The stitches need
to be just loose enough that you can
push the needle into the loop easily.

When you are starting out it is a
good idea to count your stitches at
the end of each row to check you
haven't dropped one. This is good
practice, because when you try more
complicated patterns, keeping track
of stitches and rows is a key skill.

Decorative details

Once you have made your scarf, you
might want to add extra decorative
details such as a fringe. Adding
a fringe is easy to do. Use either
the same colour wool or go for a
complementary colour. Take four or
five lengths of wool each measuring
about 15 centimetres (6 inches) long
and fold them in half. Use a crochet
hook to pull the wool through the
last row of knitting stitches to make a
loop. Pull the ends through the loop
and pull tight.

KNITTING A HAT

Once you have practised your knitting skills by making some scarves, you can move on to something more challenging. This is a simple hat to make, because once you have knitted up the pattern, you simply sew up one seam.

In this pattern, you knit two stitches together, which is shortened to "k2tog". This is a way to shape your knitting. To do this, you simply put the right needle into two stitches and knit them as if they are one stitch.

THE HAT PATTERN

You will need:

8 mm needles, Sirdar® Denim Ultra yarn.

- Cast on 51 stitches. K means knit and p means purl.
- Row 1-8 – knit
- Row 9 – knit
- Row 10 – purl
- Repeat last two rows six times
- Row 23 – (k3, k2tog) 10 times, k1
- 41 stitches
- Row 24 – purl
- Row 25 – (k2, k2tog) 10 times, k1
- 31 stitches
- Row 26 – purl
- Row 27 – (k1, k2tog) 10 times, k1
- 21 stitches
- Row 27 – purl
- Row 28 – (k2tog) 10 times, k1
- 11 stitches
- Row 29 – purl
- Cast off

To finish, sew the side seams together. Use a darning needle and matching wool. Sew along the seam using a neat overstitch. Sew the yarn in at the end of the seam and knot.

A FLOWER PATTERN

Try knitting a simple flower to decorate your hat.

You will need:

8 mm needles, yarn (you could use the same yarn as for the hat and scarf, but any yarn and appropriate size needle works), tapestry or darning needle.

There is only one row to this flower after casting on.

- Cast on 40 stitches.
- Knit 1, cast off six stitches (you now have two stitches on your right needle).
- K1, cast off six stitches (you now have four stitches on your right needle).
- K1, cast off six stitches (you now have six stitches on your right needle).
- K1, cast off six stitches (you now have eight stitches on your right needle).
- K1, cast off six stitches (you now have ten stitches on your right needle).
- Cut the wool about 20 centimetres (8 inches) from the knitting. Thread the 20-centimetre (8-inch) tail through a tapestry needle and pull that needle through each of the remaining 10 stitches on your needle from the first to the last knitted. Remove the stitches from the needle and pull tightly. Secure the ends by sewing and knotting at the back of the flower.

It's important to get the tension (tightness) of your knitting right, so that your hat is the right size. It's easy to get so involved with following a pattern that you knit too tightly. If you do this you may find that your hat is too small!

Getting it Right

DEVELOPING YOUR SKILLS

Once you have learned the basics, there are books and websites giving ideas and instructions for other projects for beginners and improvers. You may find a local group that provides classes or workshops, or simply gets together to knit. This is a fun way to get advice and inspiration from more experienced knitters.

TRY THIS!

Felting is a fun thing to do with your knitting. You put the knitted item in a hot wash and it will shrink and look like felt. You need to use 100 percent wool yarn. Experiment with small knitted squares to start with. Look for books about felting at the library or search for information on felting on the Internet.

Following a pattern

In most patterns words will be shortened. For example:

- "st" means stitch
- "cont" means continue
- "rep" means repeat.

Don't worry if this is hard to understand at first. You will soon get used to it.

There are many new words to learn, and here are some of the most common:

- Tension (also known as gauge) is how many stitches and rows you should have for every 2.5 centimetres (one inch) you knit. It is a good idea for more complex patterns to knit a sample to test that the size is correct.
- Increase (shortened to "inc") is adding a new stitch to a row to make it longer.
- Decrease ("dec") is taking a stitch from a row to make it shorter.
- Garter stitch is knitting every row.
- Stocking stitch is knitting one row and purling the next.

As you learn you'll discover new words and given time you'll soon understand what other knitters are talking about!

As you knit, mark where you are on the pattern, so that you do not lose track. If you put your knitting down it is quite easy to forget which direction you were knitting, so try to finish a row before you answer the door or the phone.

TIP

Crochet craft

A crochet hook is a useful knitting tool, and knowing some simple crochet stitches can be handy. Crochet uses one hooked needle to make the stitches.

Crochet is a great to way to make fancy edges for knitting and other decorative pieces. Turn to page 52 to find details of a website that has clear videos of all the stitches. There are also books you can use to teach you to crochet. Learn how to do single and double crochet. Practise until you are confident you can crochet each stitch well.

You can use cotton yarn to make more delicate, lace-type crochet items or trimming.

Crochet Flower

QUICK CRAFT

Use chunky wool and a large hook (size L/11) to make a crochet flower. ["Sc" means single crochet. "Dc" means double crochet.]

Make a chain of 20 stitches. Sc into 3rd chain from hook. Then sc, dc, sc, sc all in the same stitch. Sc into next chain. Then sc, dc, sc, sc into same stitch, sc into next and so on to the end of the chain.

Finish off leaving about 30 centimetres (12 inches) of free wool. Pull the wool through the last loop and knot. Roll up from one end to form a flower shape. Thread a darning needle on to the long bit of wool, and then thread the wool through the bottom of the flower (chain side) and pull tight, gathering in the bottom. Tie off. Decorate the centre of the flower with a button or bead.

Jewellery Craft

Jewellery includes decorative pieces such as necklaces, bracelets, rings, and earrings. Many techniques are used in jewellery making, some using precious metals such as gold and silver and also expensive gemstones. You can make your own jewellery using beautiful beads and wire or stringing materials. Making jewellery is versatile, creative, and fun.

A BRIEF HISTORY OF BEADS

Beads have been used all over the world for thousands of years. At first beads would have been crafted from materials such as shell, bone, or wood. In many cultures, beads are used to give information about the wearer; for instance, to show if they are married or their status in a tribe.

DID YOU KNOW?

At one time in Africa and the Americas, beads were used by European traders as currency.

Types of beads

Beads can be beautiful and **versatile**. There are hundreds of sizes, styles, colours, and shapes. How beads look (the finish) can also vary. Some beads are carved and textured while others are smooth. Some beads are transparent and some are **opaque**. Some beads have **iridescent** finishes that make them shiny like metal.

Beads are made of many different materials such as plastic, wood, metals such as tin, gold and silver, ceramic, glass, or **semi-precious stones**.

Using different beads

By experimenting you will learn how different beads can be combined together. A beginner can learn a lot by simply threading different beads on a stringing material.

A simple necklace of beads all in the same size and colour can be beautiful. However, you may find that the beads sit better with "spacer" beads between them. Spacers are narrow beads that are either plain or have simple designs. By placing spacer beads between more fancy ones, you can make the more eye-catching beads stand out.

Experiment with patterns of beads such as three of one type and four of another, and mix beads of different materials and shapes. Alternatively, you could try randomly threading a mixture of glass beads on to a string just to see how they turn out.

When you go to a bead shop, take time to feel and weigh the different materials. Glass and metal beads are generally heavier than beads made of wood or plastic. The weight of the beads is important when designing a piece of jewellery. Sometimes you need heavy beads to make a necklace hang well, but earrings made of heavy beads are uncomfortable to wear.

↓ *Beads come in a fabulous range of sizes, shapes, materials, and colours.*

MAKING JEWELLERY

You can buy jewellery kits that contain all you need to make a piece of jewellery. These kits are good for a beginner, but nothing beats choosing beads and deciding how to use them. You may be surprised how easy it is to design a simple piece from scratch.

Some striking pieces of jewellery are made from everyday objects. Some designers use ordinary household items such as safety pins and buttons to create fabulous pieces.

Different findings

"Findings" are metal pieces that hold jewellery together or in place, such as necklace clasps, earring wires, brooch backs, jump rings, and crimp beads.

- *Jump rings* are simple rings that can be opened and used to join things together.

- *Crimp beads* are soft metal beads that can be crushed, using a special tool, to secure other beads.

- *Head pins* are lengths of wire with a flat end to stop the bead falling off. They can be used to make earring dangles and pendants.

- *Earring wires* are small pieces of wire that have been formed to fit through pierced-ear holes and fasten securely.

If you are choosing earring wires, avoid the brass or plated ones as they can cause ear infections. Pay more for surgical steel or silver ones if you can.

TIP

Learn by looking at the jewellery in your home or in a shop and studying how different findings have been used.

Look and learn

It is important to use the right findings so the more knowledge you have, the more likely you are to make the right choices. Hunt out pieces of jewellery and different beads in thrift shops. You can see how jewellery is made by taking it apart and then reusing the beads and other parts to make new pieces.

Make sure the beads you choose to use have a big enough hole so you can thread them. Imagine how annoyed you'd be if you bought beautiful beads and found they were useless for your piece!

Make a simple "lariat" necklace

QUICK CRAFT

Buy a length of thin leather cord about 61 centimetres (24 inches) long. You'll need two large beads and ten smaller beads.

Make a knot about 6 centimetres (¼ inch) from one end, then thread on a large bead and make another knot to hold it in place.

Make another knot about 5 centimetres (2 inches) along and add another smaller bead and knot that in place, too.

String and knot the rest of the beads, adding the larger bead to finish.

Wear this lariat necklace by simply tying it loosely around the neck.

WIRE AND BEAD JEWELLERY

Creating jewellery with beads and wire is fairly easy to do and requires only a few tools. There are some simple techniques to learn, and then you can start experimenting.

Essential tools

- *A board* – use for cutting and glueing. This could be a piece of wood or an old chopping board.

- *A bead mat* – cheap to buy and made of special material that stops beads rolling away as you work. A good alternative is a towel.

- *Pliers* – the most useful for a beginner are round-nose and snipe-nose pliers. Buy the best you can afford.

- *Side cutters* – it's best to buy real jewellery cutters, because they are smaller and allow you to trim wire more neatly.

- *Plastic storage boxes* – clear boxes save you rummaging through containers to find beads.

Check prices on the Internet, but if you buy from a local craft store you can try out different equipment to make sure it works for you.

Getting it Right

Always use safety goggles when you are cutting wire. The pieces of wire can flick off as they are cut and could easily hit you in the eye. You can buy safety goggles cheaply from a DIY store. Always hold the end of the wire you are cutting to prevent it flicking off.

Round-nose pliers

Snipe-nose pliers

Side cutters

Choosing wire

Start with 18–20 gauge wire. The best wire for a beginner is brass. It is cheap and sold in pound coils. This means you can get plenty of practice. Memory wire is another useful material to experiment with. It is called memory wire because it is coiled into circles and keeps this shape. You can buy memory wire in sizes suitable for necklaces, bracelets, and rings.

Wire wrapping

One of the simplest and most useful techniques you can learn is wire wrapping. To practise this you will need a head pin, a bead, and pliers.

TRY THIS!

❶ Thread a bead on to the head pin. Use your round-nose pliers to grip the wire just above the bead. Push the wire with your finger, and bend it to a 90° angle.

❷ Using your round nose pliers, grip the wire just above the bend.

❸ Then wrap the wire round the pliers until it is pointing down.

❹ Wind the wire around the wire at the top of the bead to make a loop. Hold the loop in the pliers and wrap the wire around the headpin, wrapping away from you.

❺ Snip off the extra wire as close to the bead as you can. Squeeze the wrapped wire gently with your snipe-nose pliers to make sure the wire end does not stick out.

MAKING NECKLACES AND EARRINGS

This page will give you ideas about how to make pieces of jewellery using some of the techniques you have learned. Don't feel you have to copy anything exactly – unless you want to, of course! You can always add extra beads or use different findings to make the pieces your own.

You will need:

- Earring wires
- Head pins
- Jump rings
- A selection of beads
- Stringing material
- Clasps

Add more beads

Add a mixture of beads to your head pin, to make earring dangles. To make simpler earrings, you can just make a loop above the bead, making sure the end of the wire folds snugly back to the bead. This is similar to the wire-wrapping technique, but you don't wrap the wire.

Making a wire-wrapped necklace

Use the wire-wrapping technique from page 31 to make a pendant necklace. Choose a large bead and think about adding smaller beads above it on the head pin.

Then choose your stringing material. You could simply string your pendant onto a silver chain, or you could cut a length of leather cord.

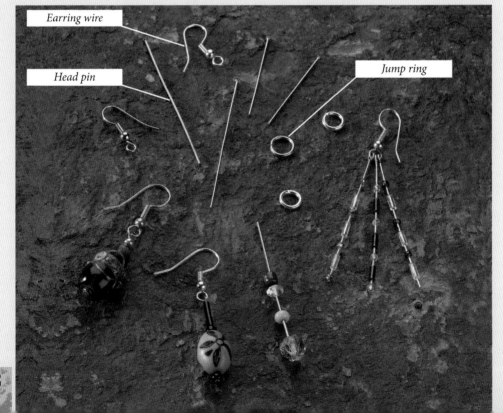

Earring wire

Head pin

Jump ring

Perfecting techniques

If you want your pieces of jewellery to look neat and professional you will need to practise your wire-handling techniques. You may find it helpful to practise using the pliers with odd lengths of wire. Twist the wire this way and that to create coils and loops and form different patterns and shapes. Practise the wire-wrapping procedure over and over until you thoroughly master the skill.

After a while you will become more skilful at using the pliers and you will find that you become more confident when working with wire.

Learning more

The examples we have shown you in this book cover the simplest forms of jewellery making. Obviously there are many more techniques to learn. One of the best ways to pick up new skills is to decide on a particular item you would like to make, then do some research in books and on the Internet to see if anyone else has done something similar. Most craftspeople are happy to share ideas and give hints and tips on techniques.

Check your local listings or on the Internet to find courses and workshops in your area. These offer great opportunities for swapping ideas, using new tools, learning new skills, and trying out different materials.

Using jump rings

TRY THIS!

Jump rings are useful for joining parts together. Use jump rings to add bead dangles to necklaces. Attach a jump ring to a charm to add the charm to a necklace.

When you open a jump ring, use two pairs of pliers to twist the two ends in opposite directions to open it. Never pull it apart to open the circle, because this will distort the shape and it will be difficult to restore it.

PAPER CRAFT

Paper is made of plant fibres. The word paper comes from the Egyptian word papyrus. The ancient Egyptians made paper by glueing small pieces of papyrus reed together to form sheets. Today most paper is made from wood pulp.

TYPES OF PAPER

Paper is a fantastic **medium** for craft because it is cheap, easy to work with, and versatile. Tissue paper, wrapping paper, coated and printed papers, handmade paper, **newsprint**, and **parchment** are all different types of paper.

↓ *Feel different pieces of paper between your fingers: some are smooth, some are bumpy, some are bendy, and some are stiff.*

The nature of paper

As paper is formed, the fibres line up in parallel. This is called the **grain**. Paper is more flexible along the line of the fibres than across them. Understanding the nature of paper and how it is made will help you when you are using it.

If you tear a piece of paper you can see the fibres underneath the smooth surface. Try tearing it in different directions to see if it looks different. If you hold any paper up to the light, you can see the texture of the fibres.

Paper craft tools and equipment

Working with paper requires very few tools. However, it is important to choose good quality tools. Small, sharp scissors will make all the difference to a paper cut-out. PVA glue can make some thin papers wrinkle and may spoil a **collage**.

These are the essential tools for working with paper:

- *Scissors* – large scissors are best for cutting large sheets of paper. Use small scissors with pointed blades for cutting out small pictures and shapes.

- *Craft knives* – a good quality knife with a replaceable blade is best. Make sure you change the blade regularly, as a sharp blade is generally safer to use than a blunt one.

- *Cutting mat* – self-healing cutting mats are expensive, but they are designed for the job and make cutting safer because the surface is non-slip. A cheap plastic chopping board is a good alternative.

- *Glue* – PVA or white glue is useful for most paper crafts but it is not ideal for thin papers because it can cause wrinkling. Glue sticks are great for neatly sticking down pieces of paper or thin card and stronger glues can be useful for adding decorations. A plastic glue spreader can be handy for bigger jobs. Choose glues that are solvent-free.

Getting it Right

If you are using a craft knife, use a metal ruler. A plastic ruler will just get scratched and rough, which will make it useless for other tasks. Always replace your craft knife blade as soon as it becomes blunt. Not only will a sharp blade give you a better cut, but it is also safer because it is less likely to slip around on the paper.

Cutting safely is an important skill when you are using sharp scissors and craft knives. When you are using a craft knife, always cut away from yourself.

DIFFERENT EFFECTS

There are many exciting ways that you can experiment with paper craft just by using different papers that you have at home. For instance you can use old cards, pictures from magazines and newspapers, torn pieces of wrapping paper, and pretty packaging. Old maps and sheet music make great decorative finishes.

Working with papier maché

Papier maché is a French term that means chewed-up paper. A paper pulp is made by tearing paper into small pieces or strips and soaking them with glue. The strips are then stuck together in layers, and form a material that is a little like a lightweight plaster. If you are using old newspaper, tear the strips rather than cutting them with scissors. This will achieve a smoother surface.

Make a carnival mask

Make a mask by blowing up a balloon so that it is roughly the size of your head. Tear up newspaper strips and soak each strip in a liquid glue solution. Cover one side of the balloon with layers of paper strips; six or seven layers should be enough. Leave to dry and then pop the balloon with a pin.

For a half-face mask, cut out eye holes and a curved shape for the bridge of your nose. For a full-face mask, you can use paper pulp mix — toilet tissue is the quickest and easiest to use — to mould features on to your mask. Leave to dry, then paint and varnish. You can decorate your mask with sequins, glitters, or even coloured feathers.

QUICK CRAFT

Creating a collage

Collage comes from the French verb *coller*, which means "to stick". Collage is glueing pieces of paper or other materials to a piece of card or canvas to create a picture or a piece of art. Materials used can be newspaper clippings, pieces of fabric, coloured or hand-made papers, or photographs. You can use collage to decorate something ordinary, such as a shoebox, or to make fabulous greetings cards for family and friends.

TIP

When you are cutting something out, turn the object you are cutting into the scissors whenever possible, rather than turning the scissors.

Decorating with decoupage

Decoupage comes from the French word *decouper*, which means "to cut out". Decoupage is a popular and easy way of decorating boxes or items of furniture by carefully cutting out images or patterns from paper (such as floral gift-wrap paper) and glueing them on. Paint effects are often used to add details. Layers of varnish are then applied to the finished item. The varnish not only provides a tough coating, but also disguises the fact that the images are stuck on. The paper cutouts can look as if they have been carved or painted. A wide range of patterned papers especially for decoupage can be bought in good craft shops, or on the Internet.

Decoupage can transform a simple item into something beautiful and unique.

SCRAPBOOKING

Scrapbooking is collecting together photographs and other **memorabilia** into a decorated album. Writing the notes to accompany these items – for instance, funny comments, explanations, dates, or captions – is called journaling.

Planning an ideas scrapbook

An ideal scrapbooking project for a craftsperson is an ideas book where you can store all your sources of inspiration. It's a great place to keep interesting pieces of fabric, doodles of designs, newspaper and magazine clippings, and photos. You can also staple resealable bags to some of the pages to store items such as beads, buttons, and lace.

Assembling materials

To start you off, you will need:

- A spiral bound book with unlined pages
- Resealable bags
- Background papers
- Scissors
- Pencils and pens
- A selection of paints
- Glue, or glue sticks
- A selection of different coloured card
- Double-sided sticky tape.

TIP

Don't crowd too much on each page. If the background is too busy the photographs get lost. The decorative details should enhance photographs, not distract from them. Add an envelope or a paper pocket to a page to store odds and ends that won't fit on the page.

Laying out the pages

The first step is to gather all the materials, cuttings, scraps, sketches, doodles, and other odds and ends that you want to keep in your ideas book. Some things may look good grouped together by colour. Plan some pages as mood boards showing colours, styles, or fashions that you like.

If your ideas scrapbook is for knitting, add yarn samples, or pictures of garments or accessories you like. If it's for needlecraft, stick in pictures of projects you would like to make in the future, and fabric scraps.

You might want to use your ideas book as a record of things you have made so you can look back through and think about what worked well. However, you should also enjoy flicking through it as a source of inspiration.

Planning a scrapbook layout

❶ Buy acid-free papers to preserve photos and other **souvenirs**. Photographs that are kept in an acid-free environment will not fade.

❷ Choose a theme for each page or group of pages. Group photos that show a particular bunch of people or the various stages of an event such as a holiday or a prize-giving.

❸ Decide on the colours that work best with the photos on each page of your album.

❹ Write notes so that you know how much journaling you want to include.

❺ Decide which photos you are going to include on each page. Sort through any other relevant memorabilia such as tickets, postcards, or newspaper cuttings that you may want to add.

❼ Crop or trim photos or images to lose anything that isn't important. Focus on the subject of each page.

❽ Photos can be mounted using corner mounts, adhesive dots, or acid-free glue. To frame photos, use mats — pieces of thick paper or card a little bigger than your photo.

❾ Choose **embellishments** such as stickers, stamps, and rub-ons to decorate your pages.

ORIGAMI

There is some debate about the origins of origami, the ancient art of paper folding. Some people believe that it originally came from China and was taken to Japan, while others think it is of Japanese origin. Origami is usually made using a sheet of square paper, with colour or patterns on one side only. There are thousands of different objects and decorative items that can be made simply by folding paper. You can buy books or search the Internet for ideas and instructions on how to create origami objects, from simple paper planes to elaborate sculptures. See page 43 for an origami gift idea.

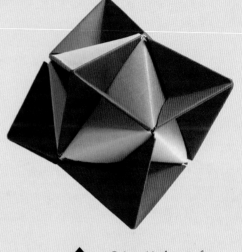

Origami is the art of transforming square, flat pieces of paper into an endless variety of three-dimensional shapes.

Origami photo frame

QUICK CRAFT

If you want to give a photograph to a friend or relative, a few simple origami folds will frame it beautifully for you. Cut a square of wrapping paper. Turn it pattern side down and fold in half, corner to corner one way and then the other. So you have two fold lines diagonally across the paper. Now fold each corner to the middle point and fold back again. Now fold each corner up to the crease made by the previous fold. Finally fold each side up so you have four straight sides. Put a dab of glue on the back of the photograph and position it in the middle of the frame. Add glue to the frame sides and stick them down.

Saving paper

Save old cards that you like and pictures from magazines, calendars, newspapers, or catalogues. Keep leftover wallpaper, scraps of wrapping paper, stamps, stickers, leaflets, or packaging with interesting designs. Remember that almost anything made from paper can be used and recycled into something new.

When using paper be creative and flexible. Don't feel you have to follow the materials listed for a project exactly. Experiment by choosing a different type or texture of paper or another colour. You can create something original and unique by trying out something new. It may not always work out well, but you will learn by experimenting and making mistakes.

Paper beads

You can make beautiful beads from pieces of paper. See the chapter on jewellery making for ideas on how to string your beads.

❶ Cut or tear strips of paper. Tearing paper will give your beads a more interesting texture.

❷ Wind the paper strip tightly onto a knitting needle or an unfolded paperclip, depending on how big you want the hole to be. Use glue to fix the paper in place. Slide your bead off the paperclip or knitting needle.

❸ Tearing the paper into different shaped strips will produce different shaped beads.

Some Gift Ideas

By making your own gifts you are using your creative craft skills to produce something completely unique. Think about the person you are making the gift for, and of ways you can make it special and personal for them. You don't have to spend lots of money; taking time and effort to make a homemade gift shows that you care.

THE PERSONAL TOUCH

Making a special and personal gift can be as simple as buying a packet of your grandma's favourite tea and putting it in a basket with some homemade biscuits wrapped in homemade paper and ribbon. Alternatively, you could buy a packet of seeds and paint some small terracotta pots for a friend who loves gardening.

Making cards

Making cards is easy, but you need to make sure that the cards look neat and professional. Use a craft knife, a ruler, and a cutting mat to cut out your rectangle of card, and fold neatly.

The simple cards in the photo on the right were made using coloured card, a flower-shaped hole punch (available in good craft shops), some crystals, glue, and coloured pens. However, you could try to think up some original card designs of your own:

- Cut letters from magazines and newspapers to spell out a message on the front of your card.

- A simple square of beautiful patterned fabric or paper, glued to black card.

- A paper egg shape decorated with patterned circles for Easter.

- A house shape decorated with paper pieces for a new home card.

- A flower made from a button and paper petals.

- A collage card.

Origami gift box

Make this simple origami gift box.

❶ Cut a square piece of coloured paper. Fold in half, from top to bottom and half again from side to side, to make two creases.

❷ Using the creases as a guide, fold the four corners into the centre.

❸ Using the creases as a guide, fold the top into the centre, and the bottom into the centre, then unfold to show two creases.

❹ Fold the left and right sides into the centre, and unfold to show four creases.

❺ Unfold the top and bottom corners.

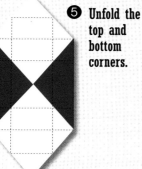

❻ Fold up the left and right side.

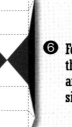

❼ Push in the corners, and fold down the top into the box.

❽ Repeat with the bottom.

❾ Your finished box.

Make a slightly bigger box and use as a lid.

DECORATING PICTURE FRAMES

Take a tired old wooden picture frame and transform it by adding decorative details.

Look out for cheap old wooden picture frames at car boot sales or charity shops. Or you may have old frames at home that you can use, but don't forget to check with an adult first! Choose quite thick, flat frames. If the frames are too thin, or textured, they will be fiddly to decorate and won't look so good.

Some picture frame variations:

- Use the collage technique to cover the frame with foil or sweet wrappers. Cut the wrappers into small squares. Spread glue on a small section of the frame at a time and overlap the wrapper squares so the frame is covered. Smooth each wrapper carefully for a professional finish.

- Paint the frame with **matt** white paint. Then use a stencil to sponge print simple shapes around the frame. To make a stencil, cut a simple shape, such as a heart or a circle, out of card. Dip a sponge in paint and dab over the stencil. Move the stencil and repeat.

- Cut out words or phrases that mean something to the person you are giving the frame to. Stick them around the frame and seal them with an acrylic matt varnish.

TRY THIS!

Black and white button frame

You will need:
- **Black gloss paint**
- **Sandpaper**
- **Small white buttons**
- **PVA glue**
- **Odds and ends of thick, brightly-coloured yarn.**

Clear your work surface and protect it with old newspaper. Collect all the things you need.

Rub the frame with sandpaper to roughen it. Then paint the frame front and back. Leave the paint to dry for a couple of hours.

Dab a generous blob of PVA glue on to each button and press it on to the frame. Start with one at each corner, and then add three or four down each side.

This simple black and white button frame is striking, but if you want to add some colour, trickle swirls of PVA glue between the buttons, and stick pieces of yarn over the swirls.

This frame was made by spreading a layer of glue over a painted wood frame. Shells collected from a beach were pressed into place. Then sand was sprinked on to cover the glue and fill the gaps.

GIFT WRAPPING

An effective way to personalize any gift is to make or customize your own gift-wrap paper. Alternatively, you could try making simple boxes (see page 47) or customize plain bags to make a gift extra special.

Print it yourself

One of the simplest ways to print paper is to make a potato stamp. First, cut a potato in half. Then draw a simple design on the potato. Cut away the potato around the shape. Paint your shape with coloured, acrylic paint and stamp it on to the paper.

Potato printing is a quick and easy way to make your own Xmas gift-wrap paper. Keep the shape simple, and use gold or silver paint for a festive finish.

You can also make a stamp by cutting out a shape from a piece of card or a piece of foam or felt. Stick the shape to a small square of wood.

Print your shapes on to plain brown parcel paper, leftover plain wallpaper, graph paper, or sheets of newspaper.

Making gift bags

Plain brown paper bags can be made into cool gift bags. Print a pattern using ideas from the paper printing section. Or use paper shapes, stickers, sequins, beads, or buttons to decorate the bag.

Gift Box

Covering a shoebox or other lidded box with gift-wrap or wallpaper is a quick and effective way to make a gift box.

QUICK CRAFT

❶ Place the box lid on the paper, and cut around it leaving about 5 centimetres (2 inches) to spare all the way around.

❷ Fold the paper up two opposite sides first and tape in place inside the box.

❸ Fold and smooth the paper on the other sides to fit the paper neatly over the box, and tape in place.

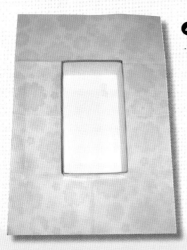

❹ Then cut out paper to fit the box, and cover in the same way.

Exploring your creativity through craftwork is fun and rewarding, and will teach you a range of useful skills. A craft could become a lifelong hobby or you could even turn it into a way of making a living. Many successful craftspeople have started out by making items for friends and family. They then discovered they could sell their work on a larger scale and developed their own small businesses.

DEVELOPING SKILLS

One of the best ways to improve your craft skills is to go to classes and workshops. There you will get an opportunity to exchange ideas with other students, try out new tools, and learn new techniques from experts.

Careers in craft

Many jobs and careers involve craft skills. For example, if you find that you excel at sewing, you could look towards a career in fashion or theatrical costume design.

Craft for fun!

This book has given you just a brief "taste" of some the crafts you can try. There are many, many others to be explored, such as woodwork, pottery, basket-making, weaving, mosaic, metalwork, and ceramics. If you find that knitting or needlework make you feel "all fingers and thumbs", then don't worry, there is sure to be another craft that is right for you. Remember, the fun is in the making, so don't be afraid to experiment. Learn from your mistakes – but above all, enjoy yourself!

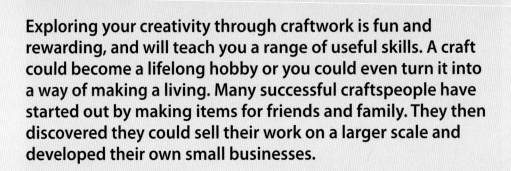

This beautiful brooch was created by an Egyptian craftsman in 1300 BCE. Visiting museums to look at examples of craftwork is a great way to get ideas and inspiration.

Quiz

ARE YOU THE CRAFTY TYPE?

1) What is a craft?
a) Making something useful or decorative by hand, using simple tools.
b) Something that is usually fiddly, frustrating, and difficult to do.
c) An activity for a rainy weekend.

2) What do you do when you make a mistake?
a) Scream, blame the tools, and throw it all in the bin.
b) Work out what went wrong and do it all again more carefully.
c) Carry on and hope no one notices the lumps and bumps.

3) What is a colour wheel?
a) A chart showing the relationships between colours.
b) Some sort of design tool.
c) A pretty circle with different colours.

4) How do you usually feel when you finish a piece of craftwork?
a) A little disappointed. It hasn't turned out quite right.
b) Really pleased with it and keen to begin work on something else and learn some new techniques.
c) Bad tempered and fed up with fiddling with it.

5) If you decide to make a crafty present for a friend, how do you start?
a) Read lots of magazines and study craft websites for ideas. Then spend time planning what to make before you start.
b) Buy a kit that has step-by-step instructions and all the materials you need.
c) Rush out to buy all sorts of expensive tools and materials, then start work straight away.

6) How do you finish a piece of craftwork?
a) Somehow you never seem to get around to finishing it. The project lies around the house for weeks, and gets forgotten.
b) As neatly as possible, but it's only a present for a friend and he won't mind if it has the odd frayed edge.
c) Very carefully; the finishing touches can make all the difference.

7) What is the best part about craft?
a) You can save money by making cheap gifts.
b) It's a good excuse to buy lots of new equipment.
c) Experimenting and practising to develop your skills and learn new techniques.

8) What is the most important thing to remember about tools?
a) Pick the right tools for the job and use them safely and well.
b) Buy the most expensive.
c) You can blame them for anything that goes wrong.

QUIZ RESULTS

ARE YOU THE CRAFTY TYPE?

For page 49

If you chose answer a) score 3.

If you answered b) score 1.

If you answered c) score 2.

2 a) 1 b) 3 c) 2

3 a) 3 b) 2 c) 1

4 a) 1 b) 3 c) 2

5 a) 2 b) 1 c) 3

6 a) 1 b) 2 c) 3

7 a) 2 b) 3 c) 1

8 a) 1 b) 3 c) 2

If you scored between 20 and 24:
Intricate craftwork doesn't hold your interest for long. You tend not to have the patience for the type of craftwork that requires precision and attention to detail. Shopping for materials and tools is usually more appealing than actually making something. This doesn't mean that you are not creative, but you may find you prefer art forms such as painting, sculpture, or woodcarving where you can express your creativity more freely.

If you scored between 13 and 19:
You enjoy doing crafts from time to time but you are not really interested in learning about craft in any detail. Craft is a hobby that is fun and relaxing for rainy days and weekends. You get pleasure from making things for yourself and other people and friends, and relatives appreciate the time and effort you take to make gifts. However, that doesn't mean you can't enjoy developing your skills and learning more, and you will have a hobby that will give you a life-time of pleasure.

If you scored between 8 and 12:
You may be a skilled craftsperson in the making. You enjoy intricate work and you like to do a good job, no matter how long it takes. This is a useful attribute for a craftsperson, but take care not to become overly obsessive about tiny details. If you feel craft might be something you could make a living from, read as much as you can about the crafts that interest you to find out about jobs and careers in related fields. Sign up for workshops and courses so that you can develop your knowledge and improve your techniques.

⟨20⟩ Things To Remember

1 As a beginner, choose quick and easy projects to give you a sense of achievement and build confidence.

2 Remember that making mistakes is part of the learning process.

3 Experiment with different materials and fabrics. You will learn by trial and error what works and what doesn't.

4 If you want your craftwork to look professional, keep practising your techniques to perfect them.

5 A skilled craftsperson uses the right tools, and uses them safely and well.

6 Preparation and planning are important. Clear a workspace and make sure you have the correct tools to hand.

7 Have a clear plan or design to work to.

8 Keep your mind open to new ideas. Experiment, think, plan, doodle, and play around with ideas.

9 Keep it simple. Simple designs are often the strongest.

10 Save and store pictures and sketches of anything you like; you don't need to know how you will use them.

11 Keep an ideas notebook to inspire you.

12 Make notes on each project to remind you what worked well.

13 Seeing how other people have used materials and colour will help you decide what might work for you.

14 Understanding a colour wheel, and colour similarities and differences is important for making colour choices.

15 Share ideas with other craftspeople.

16 Go to workshops and classes to exchange ideas and learn from experts.

17 Cutting safely is an important skill when you are using sharp scissors and craft knives. When using a craft knife always cut away from yourself.

18 When you are cutting something out, turn the object you are cutting into the scissors whenever possible, rather than turning the scissors.

19 Always use safety goggles when you are cutting wire.

20 As you knit, always mark where you are on the pattern, so that you do not lose track.

Further Information

BOOKS

Generation T, Megan Nicolay (Workman Publishing, 2006)

In Stitches, Amy Butler (Chronicle Books, 2006)

Jewellery Making: A Complete Course for Beginners, Jinks McGrath (Apple Press, 2007)

Making Stuff: An Alternative Craft Book (Black Dog Publishing, 2006)

ReadyMade: How to Make (Almost) Everything, Shoshana Berger and Grace Hawthorne (Thames and Hudson, 2006)

Second Time Cool, Anna Stina Linden Ivarsson, Katarina Brieditis, Katarina Evans (Annick Press, 2005)

The Impatient Embroiderer, Jayne Emerson (Rowan Yarns, 2006)

WEBSITES

http://www.lsew.co.uk/kids-p-00035.htm
If you love sewing, this is the site for you! There are a host of different clothing and craft projects for you to try.

http://www.recyclezone.org.uk/az_makepaper.aspx
A site that teaches you how to make recycled paper.

http://www.origami-club.com/en/
This site has lots of ideas for things to make using origami. These are demonstrated with either diagrams or animation.

http://learn-to-knit.com/Index.htm
For instructions and help with knitting for both left- and right-handers.

http://www.learndirect-advice.co.uk/helpwithyourcareer/skills/
This quiz helps you to assess your skills and interests.

http://www.ukscrappers.co.uk
Find out more about scrapbooking.

ORGANIZATIONS

Crafts Council
44a Pentonville Road
Islington
London
N1 9BY
http://www.craftscouncil.org.uk/

The national development agency for contemporary crafts in the UK. The council provides support and advice for craftspeople, as well as running training programmes and staging events and exhibitions where craftspeople can exhibit and sell their products.

Victoria and Albert Museum
Cromwell Road
South Kensington
London SW7 2RL
http://www.vam.ac.uk

This great museum is a "must visit" for anyone interested in art and crafts. Check out the V&A website to find out more about the museum's huge collections of beautifully crafted artefacts ranging from textiles, fashion through the ages, jewellery and accessories, through to ceramics, glassware, and metalwork.

GLOSSARY

artificial made by people (opposite to natural)

artisan person who does skilled work with their hands

batik method of making patterns on cloth using wax and dye

batting soft material used for stuffing or padding

blended mixed together

bobbin part of a sewing machine on which thread may be wound to be used to sew

collage art form in which materials such as paper, cloth, or string are stuck onto a surface

complementary things that work together in a useful or attractive way

currency money of a country

customize make or change something

embellishment something added to make an object more beautiful or interesting

enamel glass-like paint that forms a shiny surface when dry

grain natural patterns in the surface of paper, wood cloth, etc.

graphic related to drawing or printing

iridescent having bright colours that change when moved

linen strong cloth that is woven from the fibres (thread-like material) of a plant called flax

matt surface colour or paint that is not shiny

medium material used in art or craft

memorabilia objects that are collected because they are to do with a person or event

natural fibre thread-like material made from plant or animal products

newsprint cheap, low-quality paper used to print newspapers

opaque something that light cannot shine through

parchment high-quality paper made to look like old fashioned parchment that was made with the thin, dried skin of animals

primary colour one of three colours, which in paint, etc. are red, yellow, or blue, that can be mixed together to make any other colour

proportion the number or size of something when compared to the whole

secondary colour colour made by mixing together primary colours

semi-precious stone shaped piece of stone or rock used for making jewellery that is not valuable enough to be a gemstone such as a diamond or a ruby

silk delicate, soft fabric made from a thread made by silkworms

slip knot type of knot that is easily untied and that forms a loop that can be made smaller or bigger

souvenir something you buy or keep to remember a holiday or special event

tie-dye method of making patterns in cloth using string, knots, and dye

versatile can be used in many different ways

Index